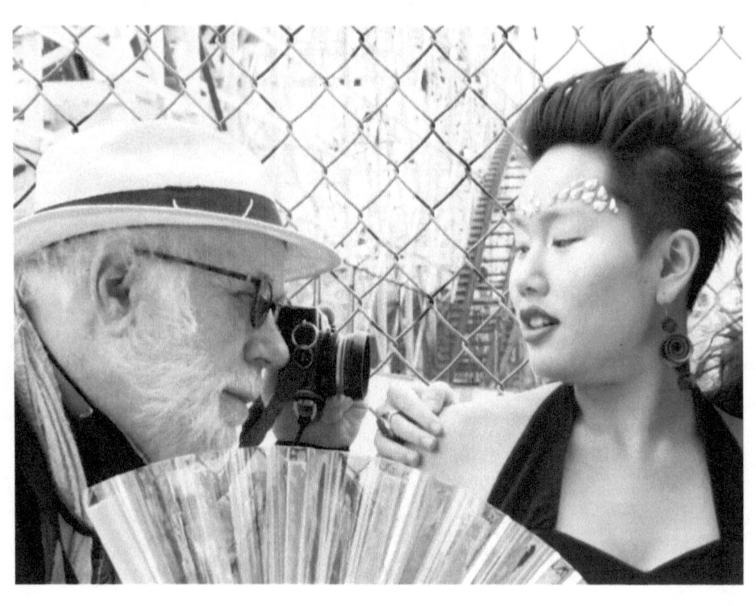

Mirrors and Smoke

How I Became a Photographer

Robert Dunn

A Coral Press Arts original

Published by BookLocker.com, Inc., Trenton, Georgia.

Printed on acid-free paper.

ISBN: 978-1-935512-57-8
Library of Congress Control Number: 2022944686
Manufactured in U.S.A.
1 3 5 7 9 10 8 6 4 2
BookLocker.com, Inc. 2023
First Edition

Cover Design: Jake Chill
Cover Photograph: Robert Dunn
Author Photograph: Sandra Wong Geroux

www.ecstaticlightphoto.com

To my father, Gerry Dunn, who would be pleased, if not astonished, that I finally became a photographer.

HONESTLY, I HAVE NO idea how I became a photographer.

O.K., it's probably a good idea not to trust anyone who begins a sentence with *honestly*, but that's just the way the first sentence came to me; and the longer I write and take photos, the more I trust what simply comes to me. What's unavoidable, what's simply there. And it's true: I really don't know how I became a photographer. Indeed part of the reason to write this book is to go over what happened, to talk about how I came to take pictures (and perhaps capture how you, if you're reading this, came to love your own photographs). Also how I got reasonably good at it, and became inspired enough to set down my tale.

I do know how I became a novelist, which I've been for all of my adult life. I was eighteen and sitting on a beach in San Diego, California, reading *Moby Dick*, when I came to a sentence so astonishing and beautiful I actually saw light pour down from the heavens. Yes, a sheet of sparkling light flowing down above me. I don't know how else to explain this other than as a religious experience, light ecstatic, the power and magic of words opening up new visions, new worlds.

I began to write back in those late-teenage years with new fervor, though it wasn't for another near decade until I actually completed a novel. Back in those early days simply filling up pages was a tough, hard climb. The blank page of paper sitting in my typewriter (just the same as the blank page on my computer today) ... what do I do? Where do the words come from? The story? Characters? Sentences then paragraphs?

I can't recall all the feints and starts, just that I somehow trained myself all those years ago to get up each morning and write. No matter what. Cross-legged on the floor, my typewriter on a turned-to-its-side speaker cabinet, when I was poor and lost between college and grad school. Then at my desk in my first New York City apartment, when I moved there in my mid-twenties and ended up in a turn-of-the-19-century three-room tenement in the East Village, bathtub in the kitchen, for $90 a month. Yes, ninety dollars a month rent. It was a wonderful flat most of the time, the whole top of the Empire State Building gleaming out my front window, though there were times when the heat went out in winter, and to keep writing I'd have to run my hands under hot water in the sink to warm them up enough to hit the keys of my typewriter.

(Curiously, my apartment, at least all the actual fixtures and furniture in it, ended up as a set in Stanley Kubrick's final film, *Eyes Wide Shut*. Long story short: I was being booted out for no longer actually living there, the landlord was going to gut the place to refurbish it, and a production assistant for the film who had somehow photographed the apartment, catching Kubrick's interest, bought everything in it for $100 and had it shipped to England, where it ended up as the set for the prostitute Tom Cruise has an affair with. Yep, my sink, my stove, my cabinets ... just not my flimsies hanging above the claw-foot tub.)

The apartment, of course, didn't make me a photographer, though being a writer possibly did. I've always seen the best photobooks as a form of literature, and I try to bring my own understanding of how I write novels to every photobook I create.

What do the two disciplines share? At bottom, the job of a novelist, after telling a good story and creating strong characters, is to make us take in the world as richly as possible: all the creatures in it, the good and the evil, and all the complexities in-between. As Joseph Conrad put it: "My task is to make you hear, to make you feel, and, above all, to make you see. That is all, and it is everything."

Likewise with the serious photographer. The task is just that: to use our images to rouse all the senses; yet above all, to make us see.

I recall a lunch years ago with the then Knopf editor, later *New Yorker* magazine poetry editor, Alice Quinn. I was still in my twenties, and doing everything I could to become a better writer. I told

Alice, "I think I'm starting to see not only just what's in front of me, but also what's behind that." I moved my hands in a circle. "I'm starting to see the whole thing."

Alice simply nodded and said, "Good."

How do you see not only what's in front of you? How about imagination. Obviously, imagination is key for a fiction writer, because you're telling stories that only exist in your own mind, inventing nearly everything as you go along. I don't think most photographers think about their craft this way. They see their task as taking a picture of what's before them. I mean, what else can you do? You move the camera, focus the lens, set the aperture, snap the shutter; what you or the camera is pointed at is what you get.

So where does imagination come in?

The lesson I learned from Alice Quinn was to see not just what's there but what *could* be there. To see around corners. To see shadows and depth. Above all, to imagine what's about to happen so you can photograph what does happen.

To imagine worlds, then fill them.

That's what I'm always trying to do with my photography. In my shots, I often like a dreamy quality, something Impressionistic, even Expressionistic (using art history terms cautiously). On the street I'm always trying to be ahead of the shot, anticipate it if I can, or at least be ready and fast enough to capture the most interesting photograph possible.

In my work, I'm not imagining something then setting out physically to create it so I can shoot it. My work is not that realistic or rational. No, this quality of imagination in photography is something more mystical, fluid, amorphous, evanescent.

What it comes down to is that the more of what's before me that I can see, or simply intuit, the more I can get into a photograph. What I'm calling imagination is the ability to see all that is *not* there in the midst of what is.

If by following imagination the photo is richer, more magical and interesting, then I'm doing my job.

I'm making you see.

*****

I MOVED TO NEW YORK CITY in the mid-'70s, when the city was broke and falling apart. I wrote about this time in my novel *Savage Joy*, my most autobiographical work. It was hard times in New York town, as Bob Dylan put it. Crime was everywhere, there were whole blocks of the city you simply did not walk down. Ditto parks, even major ones such as Bryant Park behind the New York Public Library, and Union Square on 14th Street. You simply did not go there.

And everywhere you did go, you kept your eyes moving, looking for threats, danger, crime. You had to have a good street sense, or you might as well move back to the suburbs. (A lot of people had: From 1970 to 1976, the New York City population had dropped by 5.6%, over 400,000 souls—and created a lot of open apartments.) With a mix of luck and savvy, I never got robbed or mugged. At parties back then most conversation revolved around personal crimes: bag snatchings, robberies at knife point, the kind of burglary when you come home and find your front door swinging wide. The worst that happened to me was an old guy tried to pee on me as I was walking down my East Village block to take the subway to work.

Which meant I was pretty damn lucky.

But I'd also picked up some street smarts. The way you did it was always to be paying attention to everything on the street, letting your eyes sweep constantly back and forth, checking out faces, groupings, postures … trying to read interest, intent, any potential threats. If you let your guard down for a moment, they'd get you … yes, they would. Walking along I would actually swing my head from side-to-side. New York City streets can be wide, there was a lot to take in. I also had to be ready to act if I saw something, to speed up, slow down, affect a wholly disinterested air or shoot out a sharp glower, always ready to move, cross the street, stop and feign looking into a shop window … all the moves that kept me from being a casualty, a victim. (I was a novelist, remember, working out my fingers more than my biceps, and not like one of my mentors, John Irving, who was a dedicated wrestler; I was more interested in avoiding trouble than seeking it out.)

So my head kept swinging, my eyes kept sweeping, taking everything in. What's the most basic quality of a good street photographer? Well, there are many, and I'll be talking about all of them in this book—imagination, as I've already touched upon; speed; fearlessness (I've learned a few things about that over the years); and simply a good eye—but I'd say most important is to see the whole street and everything going down in it at all times. There are always pictures to be taken, interesting ones, even astonishing ones, but it all comes from taking in the whole street and every person and gesture and shape filling it.

And also how it all fits together. Arguably the most important street photograph ever is Cartier-Bresson's shot of a man leaping over a puddle in Paris, "Behind the Gare St. Lazare." This is the shot in which the leaping man is perfectly reflected in the shallow water, whose farthest foot is a quick couple millimeters above the water, where the barrel hoops in the water form perfectly compatible arcs, where the crosses atop a building to the left mimic the top of the iron fence behind the water, and where—the ideal cap—there is a poster, behind and to the left of the man, of a dancer mimicking almost exactly his leap.

There is some discussion how planned this shot was, but even if the situation partially existed in Cartier-Bresson's mind before he actually shot it, he still fills the photographic frame with eerily perfect details, more than anyone else can ever hope to slip into one photograph, yet not too many, either.

Cartier-Bresson, to his bemusement, was labeled with the sobriquet the Man of the Decisive Moment, and what that means is that the most powerful street photographs are just that, a capture of a moment that is redolent of meaning, depth, inexplicable magic … that means something, is more important than other surrounding moments, that is, in that word, for better or worse, *decisive*.

I don't know that in my own street photography I'm shooting for decisive moments (I certainly wouldn't call them that), but I am taking in everything I can and flicking my camera's shutter button when I think I've stumbled upon a moment that, if I'm quick enough, will make a startling, surprising photograph. To do this I need to see everything, and then move fast enough when the constant flow of people and images before me are about to coalesce into a moment worth snapping.

I'm glad these days New York is a far safer place; that I don't have to walk down the streets worrying about the clink of brass knuckles against a belt buckle behind me, the sharp snap of a knife blade. But I am glad for what I endured those decades back for what it taught me as a photographer.

Street smarts are essential.

*****

I'VE BEEN TALKING ABOVE about my photography without saying anything further about how I even began to think about being a photographer; it's like I jumped ahead in the storyline. Well, I expect I'll be jumping around a fair amount, because this book is not an autobiography, not a how-to guide in any way; neither will it be linear in construction, nor with any kind of clear and obvious plot. It will simply get as close as I can to trying to understand how I became a photographer, and all I've learned in taking photos and writing about photobooks. I assure you it will all add up.

But, yes, before I even decided I could be a photographer, there I was in the previous section out taking pictures. Actually when I got going seriously, Cartier-Bresson and Walker Evans were key, especially a book of their work brought together under the title *Photographing America: 1929–1947*, compiled by Agnés Sire.

Photographing America … that's what I wanted to do. (Robert Frank's *The Americans* has always been my key text.) I keep the Evans–Cartier-Bresson book on the bookshelf nearest to my front door, and for my first couple years of serious street photography, every day that I went out shooting, I would pull it off the shelf on my way out the door with my camera, thumb through it, try to glean a new lesson from one or more of the classic shots. A few randomly opened pages: Cartier-Bresson's bewhiskered man in a straw hat and a MONEY ORDERS sign hung around his neck, below the admonition GET A LITTLE FUN OUT OF LIFE painted on a window; Evans's man and woman in a convertible jalopy, exactly the right startled and curious expression on their faces; Cartier-Bresson's equally curious yet wary African-American woman below a Beale Ave. street sign, her head just below that rule-of-thirds line at the bottom (composition is all!); Evans's memorable studio window, with hundreds of small portraits in its fifteen frames (you mean you can just shoot a window on the street?); Cartier-Bresson's one-legged Black man turning a corner in Brooklyn. So many great, stirring photos. Lifting it off the shelf as I was going out to take pictures always inspired me.

I was also aware I was using *Photographing America* as a talisman; just fanning its pages would set me off in the right mind-set. Because as much as having a see-everything street-smart vision was key to what I was up to, there were other things in the mix, too.

The most basic? Simply: I'm going out to take pictures.

I know, how obvious. But that's the thing, I've always loved walking the city, block after block, this neighborhood and that neighborhood; and with my love for bookstores, especially the Strand, at 12th St. and Broadway, it was always, Hmnn, I'm downtown, why don't I walk up through Soho, then keep going, hit the Strand (maybe pick up a photobook from their Rare Book Room; more on this later), then just keep heading north. It's all interesting.

When I started taking pictures, these walks became vastly more interesting. The walks weren't just pleasant strolls but creative endeavors. It wasn't just, Look at that, that's intriguing; it became, Look at that, and that, and that … and did I get that picture? Or that one? What about that one over there?

If part of the joy of a good walk are those pleasures of rhythm; and not thinking, just looking; and letting your mind be both present and not present … well, doing this with a camera as a photographer on the street simply enhances all these qualities. I'm going to the store, but I'm not simply going to the store; I'm after something far richer, creamier, delicious. I'm after the thrill of taking a vivid, unexpected photograph.

Joel Meyerowitz puts it well: "The camera is saying, 'Go, go, take me somewhere—take me on an adventure.' "

That's the difference between just a walk, and a walk with a camera. I'm on an adventure, day after day, just strolling down the street.

What could be more exciting than that.

There's also that simple joy of being fully present—actually, beyond wholly present. If a good long walk helps put you fully present in the world, then hoping to grab telling, magical moments from it makes you even more present.

Indeed, when taking photos on the street you simply cannot be too present. Let me say this again. The job is to be so fully in the street that, again, you see everything, sense everything, feel everything, and are ready at a millisecond's snap to capture in your camera the most redolent aspects of that fullness.

Yet as much as you have to be fully present, in effect to be everywhere, you also have to in equal measure simply be nowhere.

This is essential. At bottom being an artist is being both fully present and also fully not there. Wholly engaged and yet far enough back to see what that engagement is like, judge it, capture the best parts of it, then make something of it.

My best way to explain it is to be like a hummingbird's wings. That's what I always tell young writers. One wing creates; that is, puts something down on paper. The other wing destroys; that is, trims back and shapes that which you've just created.

Same with photographs. You're fully in the scene around you, this plethora of faces, gestures, objects, patterns; and yet you have to always be fully outside it, too, saying to yourself, in microsecond moments, That's interesting, that's not interesting, and, oh, wow, look, that's something I've never seen before … *snap*!

Creating then judging and destroying (or keeping).

All so fast it's a blur—that wondrous blur of inspiration and creation and achievement—all as fast as a hummingbird's wings.

*****

THESE PHOTOGRAPHIC WALKS aren't simply about the richness of self-concentration and sensual fullness, they're also an aspect of faith. In one's self, surely, but also faith in the mysterious forces of light and beauty that inspire any great art.

Let me explain. When I go out walking with my camera, I expect that I'll get good pictures, that the world, even with all its confusions, obfuscations, and orneriness will nonetheless offer up strong images, again and again if I'm attuned enough with it, and fast enough on my shutter. Toting my camera leads to a comfort in the world, not that things will necessarily go my way, but that I'll be able always to see the innumerable pictures the world contains. This is not a belief that something extraordinary will happen in front of me, for me to photograph. Indeed, the world, even here in New York City, is often a mush of tedium and dullness. Yet with my camera around my neck I keep the simple faith that I'll be able to see the extraordinary in what's in front of me, and be able to photograph it.

Even the dullest of vistas can be charged, at its corners or odd angles or behind the scrim of banality, with the exceptional. At least that's the faith I bear.

How does all this work? Again, it's all about keen and rich seeing, about noting detail, and an imagination able to tease out new ways of looking at the world even in the most commonplace of scenes. I'm not hoping for anything newsworthy to play out in front of me, a crime, a disaster, an upheaval, a conflagration. I don't usually go to places where those kinds of photos are possible. I stay close to home, wander about the city, keep my eyes moving. I'm looking for a subtle but deep flicker of human emotion. A small gesture of manifest significance. A particularly profound play of shadow and light. A concatenation of shapes and angles. A dazzle of colors.

Simply, a way of snapping the commonplace that renders it surprising and new.

There are an awful lot of photos out there. In truth, an unknowable number. That's part of the faith, that the world is teeming with fascinating, compelling, awe-lifting details. They're out there, every day, almost everywhere.

And yet my faith is not that the world will hand out photos to me; it's faith in my ability to tease out strong photos *from* the world.

This is all important, because, again, it's all about seeing. We always see the world we see. So how do we see it better? We work to divine its fullness, its breadth, its boundless depths. We learn to see what's in front of us, and what's behind. What's there and, sometimes, what's not there but which we can see anyway, or at least our cameras can, which when it comes to photography is all that matters.

That my camera will see the world's plenitude and magic, and record it.

Faith.

*****

NOW BEARING THIS FAITH day in and day out, that of course takes energy and focus; and high energy and vivid focus are always changing, fleeting at the best of times. So part of being a good photographer is knowing when you're on, when your concentration and breadth of vision is as deep and wide as it can be. It's also knowing when your concentration slips; that is, when it's time to push the camera back in your bag and go home.

Which is another joy of photography: It demands that you know yourself, how you work, when you work best, when to stick it out and when to bail. This can be called experience, perhaps even wisdom. But simply understanding how you work comes from doing the work over and over, and always paying attention to how it's going, what you can control and what you can't.

It's also all about intuition, as so much of photography on the street is.

I'm trying to remember, when I plunged deep into taking pictures, to what extent I had to learn to trust my intuition. I think I already had it; decades of writing fiction, the endless sitting before my IBM Selectric typewriter, then my first computer (a huge, metal, literally built-for-tanks Kaypro II), then my succession of Macs taught me to know when I was writing well, and when I could barely put words together. It also taught me to trust the wisps and currents and invisible threads that could yank a day's work in any number of directions. It taught me when to have a plan and when to give up any idea of a plan and just riff.

Following intuition, and trusting it, is important in fiction writing. I know it's also invaluable in music composition, and I'm sure all forms of art.

In taking photographs it's simply essential, especially on the street.

There you are out walking along, eyes alive, senses kicking. Looking, looking, looking. Each second a pure kind of existential moment, because if you think too much, you'll miss the shot. If you hesitate, you'll miss the shot. If you don't trust the camera, you'll miss the shot. (Bless digital cameras with their no cost per photo and easy ability to delete shots that disappoint. With my camera I can bang away in any direction and not think twice if all I get is a blurred wall or an empty sky.)

Let me make that last point again. You have to trust the camera. Especially in my case, since I know very little about cameras in general, and not even close to everything my own camera can do.

Does this sound like it goes against everything any photography school would teach you? Then how come I'm writing this book?

Well, that's the story that comes next: How I got into photography in the first place.

* * * * *

So remember, I'm a novelist and short story writer. I'm publishing in *The Atlantic*, *Redbook* (which garners me an O. Henry Short Story Prize), and numerous important literary quarterlies. I'm working away in the mornings at my Selectric at home, then running off to my gig at *The New Yorker* magazine, to pay the bills, and do things like accompany film critic Pauline Kael to screenings and go to parties with the likes of Norman Mailer and Kurt Vonnegut. (A dream first job, oh, yeah.)

Later I end up as the eminent novelist Bernard Malamud's assistant. (I know, he wrote the great novel *The Assistant*, but fortunately that was well before my time with him—and my job wasn't lugging in wooden boxes of groceries. No, what I did was writer's assistant work: typing letters, making runs to the post office, and accompanying Bern on long, edifying, mind-expanding walks.)

So I'm basically a literary guy, in a literary world then vibrant but, alas in the 2020s, no longer extant. I have an interest in photography, but I also don't have much money, basically enough for my cheap East Village apartment rent, groceries, and an occasional plate of pierogis at Veselka on Second Avenue. Somehow I gather enough funds to get an inexpensive Nikon, an EM model. I find

I'm singularly interested in color photography and can afford the occasional roll of Kodak Ektachrome E100 film, and then processing it into slides.

And I'm not bad. I am aware that every shot costs me money I don't have much of, so I'm careful. (A few years back I attended a terrific show at the Brooklyn Museum of up-to-then-undeveloped Garry Winogrand slides, projected one after the other on a dozen or so screens in a large room. Along with great delight at unseen shots by one of my favorite photographers, I drew a kind of personal justification: Winogrand also couldn't really afford to process all the color slides he shot, so he left them on the roll. Both that and he just couldn't stop shooting.)

With my Nikon, I do seem to have a bit of an eye for shape and color and composition. I'm out wandering with the camera on weekends, and eagerly waiting for the slides to come back, then looking at them with my pocket slide viewer. Yep, not too bad, and....

I realize I need to make prints.

Prints, it turns out, ain't cheap. Indeed, large ones are something like a quarter of my rent for just one, not to mention those pierogis.

And so my photography—well, it really was just a hobby back then, all those years ago—languishes. I keep writing, and a decade later take a swerve into music, writing songs, forming a group, Wild Mercury, that plays every couple weeks at decent clubs in NYC such as CBGB's Gallery, Arlene's Grocery, The Kitchen (alas, all departed now). That lasted until general entropy and a touch of carpal tunnel knocked out my guitar playing.

I was ready for something new.

A Friday *New York Times* review of a new camera, the Fuji X100, by David Pogue. The third paragraph in its entirety: "And the new Fujifilm X100 is—different. Quirky, amazing, baffling, out-there different."

Wow! The camera sounds fascinating. A quick mental flash: I used to be into photography all those years earlier. A quick decision: I want this camera.

A quick discovery. The then-new Fuji X100 was as hot as a new iPhone … as in, you can't buy it anywhere. I spend that morning at my then job at *Sports Illustrated* magazine refreshing the Amazon screen for the camera … and finally about noon some for sale pop up. A store that sounds familiar … oh, wait, it's in Manhattan, only a quick subway ride from my office in the Time-Life Building in Midtown.

A quick call, "Yes, we just got a shipment of X100s."

"Great. I'll be down after work to get one."

"Um, I wouldn't wait that long. I don't know if we'll still have any by the end of the day."

Quick decision. Almost lunchtime. I ask the guy to hold me one, I'll show up as soon as I can.

"Um, I'll try, but…."

I take my lunch hour early, like right then. Hit the F train at Rockefeller Center, head down to 18th Street. And … an hour later I'm back in my office with a brand-new camera.

The next day, a Saturday, I take my first serious photos in twenty-some years. The first one, nothing much, just the coffee pot on our kitchen table. Coffee for my wife and my old friend Steve, visiting from California, because I only drink tea. Then Steve and I go out to explore the city, and I take along my new Fuji.

I barely know how to operate it. I set the ISO at 400, seems like a reasonable number, everything else at Automatic, and keep my eyes moving. I do O.K., get a few not wholly uninteresting shots, nothing special, though, but it's fun … the first time I've been back in what I come to call photograph-head, that take-in-everything, see-everything way of walking about, for many many years. Steve is tolerant, happy just to be wandering the city.

We're in the Lower East Side, heading south from Delancey and Houston, just meandering, no place special; it's a lovely spring day and there couldn't be any place better than being in New York City.

Then we stumble on a place that changes everything for me.

It's an art gallery, I can't recall the name or what street it was on. Just a slender long room down in the now burgeoning east-of-Soho art belt. The show is of large copper sculptures, hanging from the ceiling, bars of copper welded together and turning slowly.

I take a picture of one, look at the back of my Fuji. O.K., there's the sculpture, with … a pleasing shimmer of light around it.

Not bad. Let's take another one.

That's when the camera goes wiggy. Beyond my control or understanding, as if it has a vision or force of its own. Quirky, amazing, baffling indeed.

The next shot captures some of the copper sculpture but what it mainly gets is a brilliant shimmer of light around it.

It's the light that catches me. It glows, it bursts, it pushes itself into the room, it lights up the whole frame I'm looking at. A warm, glowing coppery-white light.

Did I intend to take this photo? Nope. This is my first full day with this new Fuji camera, and I have no idea what I'm doing.

Did the camera want to take this picture, this frame filled mostly with an explosion of light?

Evidently. Because the next time I snap the shutter it does it again. And again. And again.

Each shot different but similar. There is even a progression here, as if the glowing light is moving, changing, growing then shrinking … as if the light has a life of its own.

I'm quietly astonished. The photos look beautiful to me. At that moment I realize that what I want most of all from my photography is to capture light. That that's what photography is, light and shadow and color and magic.

A year or so later when I set up my photobook website I call it Ecstaticlightphoto. That was the word for everything I felt that first day, and everything I wanted.

Ecstatic.

Since that first day I've taken tens of thousands of photos. Many have been realistic, sharp-in-focus; at least an equal number have been closer to an aesthetic of *Are-Bure-Boke*, as practiced by Japanese photographers such as Daido Moriyama and Takuma Nakahira whom back then I was still a good ways away from even knowing about. *Are-Bure-Boke* translates out as "grainy-blurry–out of focus." It's about expression, about light, rather than anything close to realism. A flow of consciousness rather than a document. Art not news.

I didn't know anything of this that first day. I simply knew that my Fuji, for whatever mysterious reasons, had gone haywire when I pointed it at a copper sculpture in a Lower East Side gallery and produced a photo bursting with ecstatic light.

I was hooked. Curious. Eager. Then obsessed.

There was so much to learn, so much to begin to know.

And so I discovered the photobook.

* * * * *

THAT LAST SENTENCE isn't quite accurate. It turns out I'd discovered photobooks during my first flurry of interest in photography those decades earlier with my little Nikon EM. I'd even scraped together the bucks to buy a few. I had a first edition copy of William Eggleston's *Guide* on my shelves. I like to think I had a copy of Robert Frank's *Americans*, but I'm not sure. The book I know I was most proud of owning back then was Bill Burke's *I Want to Take Picture*.

I vividly remember buying this book. This was in 1987, and I'd made my way to upper Fifth Avenue to the International Center of Photography, when it was on the corner of East 94th Street. I was blown away by the Burke show *I Want to Take Picture*, and especially by the collage-y book for sale in the museum bookstore.

I loved the black-and-white photos of Southeast Asia, where I'd already roamed around a decade earlier, and I loved the layout, the book's large size, the printing, really, everything. I know this because I remember standing in the bookshop and realizing that the cost of the book was another good portion of my monthly rent. Did I dare spend so much on just a book?

I had to. I needed to own this book. So I paid up. It wasn't long after that my first interest in serious photography waned, and I don't think I bought too many other photobooks back then, but when my fascination with photobooks returned after I got the Fuji X100, I wasn't disappointed to learn that my first edition of *I Want to Take Picture*, one of a thousand copies, was now selling for around a thousand bucks. (I met Burke a few years back at the New York Art Book Fair, and he was kind enough to sign my copy and add a bunch of quirky drawings around his signature.)

So getting interested in photobooks again wasn't maybe such a bad idea. Although I've never sold a book from my collection, it didn't hurt to realize that the best of them went out of print quickly and could easily appreciate in value.

But right then I needed photobooks to learn more about photography, what had been done, what was possible … to fill my head with ideas as I pursued further manifestations of this ecstatic light.

Fortunately, at that time ICP was at 43rd and Sixth Avenue, only seven blocks south of my day job at *Sports Illustrated.* I began to haunt the very impressive bookstore there. Likewise the second floor of the Strand bookstore. And numerous other bookstores I knew well but now discovered had good photobook collections.

I began to build a library. I carefully read *Bystander: A History of Street Photography*, by Colin Westerbeck and Joel Meyerowitz, because that was my main interest, taking photographs on the street. Then I got a copy of *The Photobook, a History*, by Martin Parr and Gerry Badger; the first volume, then quickly the second. I studied the books assiduously, dove deep into the wonders of photobooks, ones I'd heard of and many I knew nothing about. I was glad to see my few previous purchases, Eggleston and Burke, had prominent places in the Parr-Badger book. And I wanted copies of a whole lot of the others.

I was fully hooked.

And more: I wouldn't just take photos, I'd make my own photobooks. That would be my chief interest, the photobook. (I didn't yet know a thing about photography in Japan, where the photobook, not the wall print, is the primary medium. Much more to come on that.)

So I kept snapping shots, importing them all into Lightroom (which I was beginning to fumble through on my own), processing them some, learning the tools, then organizing them into different folders. I'd been a poet back in the day and didn't have trouble coming up with names for books. I started working on a few books,

books that a couple years later would be my first two books of general street photographs, *Demons and Dogs* and *Razzle Dazzle*. The fun was seeing how my disparate images would sit next to each other, begin to flow, even talk to each other. (Kind of like smashing images into one another in a poem.) I found I really enjoyed pulling groups of photos together, moving them around, in effect writing a photobook, then rewriting it, and rewriting it again—all what I'd done for years with novels. Draft after draft after draft until a book felt as finished as I could make it.

Demons and Dogs and *Razzle Dazzle* were my first go at books of my general street photography, in 2012 and '13, respectively. I sent them off to Blurb and got back an actual physical hardback book! The printing wasn't great, the paper cheap, the whole feel kind of mass market and cheesy—and too damn expensive. I only made one copy of each book, plenty enough in truth; but the photos seemed to sit within it well enough, and the whole enterprise let me know making a run of street photography photobooks was possible.

I'd already made my first serious photobook, though: *OWS*. Hardly expecting to—and with no expectations how it might be received—but … well, here's how the whole deal with that first book went down.

OWS stands for Occupy Wall Street, the two-month occupation of Zuccotti Park in downtown Manhattan, and it was going on in the fall of 2011, six months after I got my Fuji.

I first took the subway down there in late September, to donate copies of a novel of mine, *Look at Flower*, to the free library I'd heard they had there. *Look at Flower* is about a hippie chick, Flower Evans, and her adventures in 1967 with the Grateful Dead and the whole counterculture scene, and I thought it would find some readers. Indeed, Wavy Gravy said of my book, "For those youth seeking data of their elders, here lies the anatomy of a hippie chick. Check it out!"

I went to college at UC Berkeley at the tail end of the Sixties, and the first thing I noticed at Zuccotti Park was that the atmosphere there, the very air, was the closest to what I recalled from Berkeley all those decades back. It's hard to describe, but I felt I was in the same kind of space as Cal was during its own days of rage in spring 1970 … and I'd known nothing like it since. (I'm reminded of how, in the early '80s I was walking up First Avenue, around the corner from my then apartment on East 11th Street, and I heard two men walking in front of me arguing about the Vietnam War. How strange, I remember thinking. This is Reagan-Bush-Yuppie times, and somebody's still arguing as if it's 1973. How cool. Turned out the two men were the poet Allen Ginsburg and a pal.)

So there I was at Zuccotti Park, filled with protesters in tent encampments, marching about, passing out leaflets, selling buttons, doing their best to call attention to profound inequities in American class structure.

I of course had my camera with me. By this point I didn't go anywhere without it except maybe to walk the dog or get a loaf of bread from the local market. And around me I saw nothing but pictures.

I wasn't the only one with a camera, of course. This was a big news event, at a minimum; and something nobody had seen on the streets of America in decades. That first day a lot of people had cameras. (During later visits, the proportion of people there to take pictures to people actually protesting grew noticeably; a reasonable indication of when a political movement is losing potency: more observers than activists.)

I did notice one thing with the camera people, they all were shooting pretty much the same stuff.

I discovered a great lesson. All those cameras were pointed in the same direction, toward the angry yelling man, the crazily costumed kid, the flood of handmade signs, the sea of sleeping bags all spread out. They were all taking the same pictures.

My job, I told myself, was to take different ones. I'd bring my fascination with color, light, drama to what I shot. In my first picture that day the frame was two-thirds filled with crinkled blue tarp, out of which we see a man's bare calf above black socks, his hand rubbing his skin. Just that flash of human amidst the flood of color.

I kept going. Those large blue tarps fascinated me, and I took another shot with the tarp prominent, with a red blanket visible in an opening, two guys talking behind it, and—all important—a taped-to-the-tarp piece of paper with the words BECOME YOUR DREAM above a drawing of a bird and the tag "—De La Vega."

My pictures weren't all Rothko-like patterns of color, there were a lot of shots of people. As always, I tried to fill the frame in the most interesting way, with the greatest number of interesting moves and patterns, what I had learned from Cartier-Bresson. One of my favorites in *OWS* is of a man with his hands cupped before his mouth, his head dead center before a floating red balloon, a woman to the right in a yellow NEW YORK sweatshirt, the look on her face one of curiosity and startlement, and she balanced out by another woman gazing with mysterious passion almost straight toward my camera.

Not so much newsy shots as shots composed like paintings.

Though there were plenty of newsy photos, too. The panoply of characters in the square, the range of emotions, and lots of photos of the daily lives being lived outdoors in September and October in New York City.

I wasn't a journalist; usually I was down there on a long detour before teaching my New School writing course on Thursday evenings. I'd try to stop in once a week. After I found those copies of *Look at Flower* had left the on-site library, I donated a few copies of another of my novels, *Meet the Annas*.

And I kept taking photos.

I thought they were good. I believed they weren't like everyone else's photos. I knew the event itself was important, historic. I was becoming fascinated by photobooks … and knew it was time to make my first serious one, actually produced by an actual printer, Conveyor Arts across the river in New Jersey.

I sorted photos in Lightroom, moved them back and forth, then leapt into InDesign to lay out the book. It would be paperback, zinelike in honor of its subject. I did the full layout myself, designed the cover … I wasn't just a writer any longer, I was a book designer, too. I took all of it over to Jersey City on a PATH train, eating great Indian food on the way; and a few weeks later I had fifty copies of *OWS*.

I took them to the bookstores I was getting to be known at for my interest in photobooks (and no doubt my many purchases). To my unforgettable joy the store managers liked the book a lot, and took copies. Everybody did: ICP, Dashwood, the Strand. Then I went to places I wasn't at all known. Most memorable was the bookstore at the New Museum on Bowery. The manager there said, "We don't take photobooks here. We're not that kind of—" Then he looked at *OWS* and said, "But I'll take these. They're really good. I haven't seen anything like it."

The book sold, too. Soon I was into a second printing. St. Marks Bookstore, long may it live in memory, took copies, put them out prominently. Spoonbill and Sugartown in Williamsburg. The activist bookstore Bluestockings on the Lower East Side, too. Pretty much everywhere I went.

This was self-producing a photobook, and it was so easy! (Hah.)

All successes have their odd turns. The manager of the International Center of Photography bookstore told me that ICP was going to have a show of photos around Occupy Wall Street, and that I should submit some of the ones from my book. I did. They took one, the final photo in the book, blocks of red, a dangling American flag, and words stenciled on corrugated cardboard that read:

TRUE

FREE

DOM … with a big black exclamation point to the side.

What I liked about this photo was that the sign was upside down, you had to read it from the ground up, and work a little to make out what it said. Something about it being upside down added more significance, even if I couldn't explain it.

The show was to be on Governors Island, a ferry ride away from the southern tip of Manhattan. On a fall day a year from the events in Zuccotti Park I made my way to the island, then hiked all the way across it to see the show. There was my name, ROBERT DUNN, on the list of photographers with work in the show.

And there was my photo of the stenciled sign, **true free dom!** … hung right side up.

My photo, again, had the words upside down, but the curators had flipped it over so that it was easy to read. The lack of mystery, of complication, in the photo was palpable, at least to me. Here was my first photo in a major show and they'd hung it wrong.

A shrug. What can I say. There was nobody there to complain to, so, yeah, a long shrug ... and a long trip back across Governors Island, a long ferry trip, and a long subway ride home.

* * * * *

I DIDN'T STAY MAD AT ICP for long, they were carrying my book *OWS* and other books soon to come, and they'd already done me a huge good turn. I got introduced to the work of Daido Moriyama.

There was a woman who worked in the ICP bookstore, Sarah Goldberg, I was becoming friendly with. Sarah loved photobooks, and loved turning me on to ones I should know.

One afternoon she said, "Do you know Daido Moriyama?"

I shook my head. I had no idea who that was, didn't even clearly make out the syllables. This wasn't a simple American name like William Klein I could understand in a snap, this was Japanese.

Sarah led me over to the M section of the store and pulled a couple books off the shelves.

"You need to know him," she said, holding one out. "I know you'll like him. Your own photos already have some things in common."

She was right. I bought the book, then another, then ... well, I very quickly got to know the breadth of Daido's photography, and he became one of my heroes. I loved him not so much for single photographs but for the sweep of them. How each photo was interesting even if it wasn't about anything special. Most of all, how each photo was clearly taken by Daido.

That's the thing. I can't really tell you what makes a Daido photo. Sure there are certain qualities that do set them off, the high contrast, especially in black and white; the fascination with shots of full lips, and black tights on women's legs; the layers of signage; the blends and blurs of many photos, especially from his fuck-it-all *Bye Bye Photography* days; the unexpected angles on people out there on the street; the quiet wit; the way photos collage into more than just a random corner of Tokyo or Okinawa. I can go on.

At bottom, though, each Daido photo is just that, a Daido photo. He has that elusive quality of a voice or a vision singularly his own. As I talked about above, each photo anybody ever takes is a choice, this moment rather than that moment, this angle rather than that angle, this subject rather than that subject. From my own street work I know there is an infinite flow of moments—that, of course, is simply what time is—and yet you have to choose this one, not that one for your photograph.

Looked at this way, time is infinite. So much to choose from; how can you possibly go after just one moment?

There's truly only one way, and that's to trust your instinct, your intuition, your gut.

Immerse yourself as fully in the world passing by you as you can, keep your eyes moving, take it all in … and snap the shutter when it feels right. Not when you *think* it feels right, simply when it does feel right.

It should be almost as if the camera itself takes the picture. If your own brain and intentions get too involved, you'll miss the shot.

That's what Daido doesn't do. He does not miss the shot. (Or at least doesn't put the missed shots into his shelves of books.)

And that's what I learned most from Daido Moriyama. To trust myself, most of all trust my camera. Get out of its way. Just grab my shots, as Daido always grabs his.

That's where voice and vision come from. And trusting those is the whole game right there.

*****

THEN THERE'S WHAT YOU DO with the all the photos you've taken. And that concerns Daido Moriyama, too, and one of the best times ever in my world of photography: Daido's 2011 TKY Printing Show at the Aperture Gallery in New York City.

This performance mimicked the similar performance Daido held in Tokyo in 1974, also called Printing Show, in which he took over a copy shop and waited for folk to wander in. He'd run the photos of his they wanted through the machine, pull out the sheets of paper, ask them to order them, then have them choose a made-on-the-spot silk screen cover for the book, which they then took home with them (and found out that forty years later it was worth at least $100,000).

At the Aperture re-creation (also held a year later at the Tate Museum in London) the far wall was filled with fifty-four photocopied and numbered sheets. Each participant was handed a piece of cardboard with twenty boxes. You would walk up and down the wall, taking in the photos. They weren't just single photos, though, they were double-sided, so each one had two to four photos, depending on which were full spreads or two pictures per side. The idea was to choose the sheets you wanted in your own book, put their numbers in the boxes, and when you were finished, interns would take the sheets off big piles of them in the center of the gallery, then assemble your book.

In effect, you were making your own Daido Moriyama photobook. I was in heaven.

Now I've always thought of Daido as the Bob Dylan of photography. (Daido was at TKY, signing books once they were made, and I told him that's how I thought of him; he simply smiled.) So think of it this way: You're in the same room with Dylan, there are eighteen verses to "Like a Rolling Stone" laid out in front of you, and you get to pick the four you like—your own new version of the classic song—and then Bob would sing it back to you. Yeah, something like that.

I spent hours, no exaggeration, in front of the two-sided sheets of photos. Each sheet would be folded in half, so in effect there were almost infinite ways the photos in the book could be ordered and the pictures talk to each other. Four sides, a front, a middle, a back. It was like playing chess, not checkers … or maybe Go. I had to first take in all of the fifty-four sheets, get familiar with them. They were all high-contrast shots of Tokyo, of people on the street, a dog's long snout, subway passengers, a naked woman, a plane streaking through the sky; and though most were in black and white, not all of them were. One I chose was in color, a bathtub filled with water like cherry Kool-Aid. They were all classic photos from Daido's long, stirring career. So many great photos.

Once I started to get a feel for all the choices, I began to arrange them. Numbers in the little square boxes. Hmnn, maybe that photo sheet should sit next to that sheet. O.K., let's try that. Good thing they handed out pencils. I still have my note sheet with the numbers of the photos I had to have, and the order I wanted, then the next ordering, and the next … and even on the final twenty-boxed card I see I erased a couple of numbers and substituted in other spreads.

All this ordering was in my mind, of course, since I couldn't rearrange the photos on the wall. I did the best I could. In a way my own photobook-making experience has always been informed by that November Saturday. Pick photos, move them around, lock in an order, step back, walk around, get new ideas, lock in another order, then another … and finally make my book.

A deep breath, a sigh. One last look at the photo-filled wall. O.K., I guess that's it. Right? Right.

I took my sheet up to the array of tables where the interns were assembling each work. Waited a spell, then my number was called, and I went up and got the book. Got in line so Daido could sign it. (Of course he signed *TKY*, he signs everything.) Mentioned my Dylan notion, got his inscrutable smile. Then went home—

Only to discover that the interns had totally screwed up the order of the photos in the book. I'd spent like three hours working on this, and they got the friggin' order wrong. Not only that, but a lot of the photos in my book weren't ones I'd wanted at all.

I got ahold of Aperture, and to their credit they asked me to bring the book back down there, along with my sheet with the order I wanted, and they remade the book the way I'd intended.

The irony, it turns out, is that I just pulled *TKY* off my shelf and looked at it. Right now the order of sheets I chose those years ago looks kind of wrong to me. What, I picked those photos in that order? What was I thinking?

The lesson is that, as with taking photos, especially on the street, making a book is pretty much mostly intuition, and that can change over time. Though when I do look back over my own books I'm pretty happy with how they turned out. And if I'm not, I do the only thing I can: I shrug and say, Well, it made sense at the time.

Of course those are all my photos, and I never arranged one of my photobooks away from home in only a few hours.

Still, it's always good to trust your instincts, plunge as far into the moment as you can, and try not to second guess yourself. Out on the street, you can never go back and take a photo that was at best only a glimpse of a fleeting moment. It was just that, a moment; it's gone. Likewise, you should never doubt work you made in a series of other fleeting moments. It is what it is.

Printing Show was great fun; I'd love to do something like it again. Making my own photobooks, in my own order, is also great fun; and the lessons I learned that day at Aperture—take your time, trust what feels right, work on a book until it fully comes together—have informed all of the books I've made since.

*****

SO HAD I BECOME a photographer yet? I was assiduously taking pictures, my camera with me all the time. I was loading them into Lightroom when I had a good amount, doing a little digital processing to them, then sorting them into folders for potential books. Then I got the idea for a whole series of books, and an innovative way of doing them.

The title: *Angel Parade*. The idea: modeled after paperbacks from the '50s and '60s that put two books into one volume. Most of them were published by Ace publishing, starting in 1952. They were called Ace Doubles, and were mostly genre fiction, westerns, mysteries, hard-boiled pulp. You'd read the book on the front cover, then flip it over and see a whole other cover, and read that book, till both books ended in the middle.

Same with *Angel Parade*. The first was *Angel Parade: 1 and 2*. The first book was announced by one cover, the second came when you flipped the volume over. Each photo in both books was full-bleed, and spread across the gutter.

And stores took them. The Strand was even selling them in their Rare Book Room. I did *Angel Parade*s up till book ten, paused for a bit, then kept going. There are now eight separate volumes with sixteen books. I hope to get to twenty books someday, but about seven years ago I started coming up with new ideas and began making other types of books.

So was I a photographer?

I went almost everywhere with my camera. I sure took a lot of pictures. I put out books, sold books. Got to meet and know other photographers, many of whom I had great respect for. Which leads to ... well, here's my favorite Meet a Photographer story, though it hardly makes me more or less of a photographer by itself. Still, it's pretty amusing.

I'm at a gallery opening on West 23rd Street, for a Daido Moriyama show in spring 2013. I was enjoying the photos when the door to the gallery's large back office opened, and sitting at a big table was Robert Frank. I recognized his tufts of silver hair, his wise, seen-it-all mien.

I got lightheaded, tingly. I loved *The Americans*, had studied it, and I owned numerous different copies, and ... there Robert Frank was. I can't escape it, I love being a fan; I'm sure you can tell by now.

I thought about an autograph. I know, how uncool at a chic Chelsea gallery right by the High Line. But if I'm buying signed books, and proudly signing my own for people who ask, why not?

As Frank leaves the office, along with his wife, artist June Leaf, I approach him, say something like "I'm a big fan," then ask if he'd sign something for me. He blanches, actually pulls back a couple feet and throws up his hands as if I were holding him up with a gun. His wife laughs.

Frank then shoots me a look of profound disdain and begins to walk on past. I have my camera by my side and figure if nothing else I can snap a photo or two. I keep it waist-high, tilt it up, hit the shutter, then hit it again. Then Frank's gone, out into the New York City night.

A minute later I go to look how my photos came out. I push the correct button on the camera, but what I see on the back screen is nothing but black with white dots along the side.

I've told you I don't know much about cameras, and, well, here's more proof. I have no idea what I'm looking at. I get anxious. Almost all black? Some white dots? My one chance to photograph Robert Frank?

Back home I pull out the Fuji manual, see that what I'm looking at is movie mode. O.K., that makes sense. Somehow this camera with a life and sensibility of its own has shifted itself into making movies.

I hit another button, look at the screen, which starts to dance along. It is a movie, very short. Floor, floor, ceiling, floor. That's it.

Damn!

I see there's another clip. Hit the button on that, Floor, floor, ceiling, floor . . . then a man's face floats into view. It's Robert Frank.

I end up making a short photobook, *Meeting Robert Frank*. I break the three-second video down into nineteen frames, lay them out. In the first two it's just dark shapes on a white background, then a sliver of Frank's face enters the frame. He begins to fill up more of the frames, a lot of blur, some neck, ears, hair. Then he gets clearer, and fuller in the frame. I finally get a strong profile of him. Nineteen frames. That's it.

Meeting Robert Frank does well. And here's my favorite story on that. David Strettel, the owner of Dashwood Books, agrees to take a stack of the books for his store. I bring them by on a Tuesday afternoon. As soon as I walk into the store I see Robert Frank standing there talking to a few other people, including David.

David knows why I'm there, shoots me a look, *Be cool*. I smile, nod, don't worry.

The thing is, there's Robert Frank again, but that whole frisson of my first encounter has dissipated. Sure, he's still Robert Frank, but now he's just another guy, from the neighborhood (he literally lived around the corner), visiting a photobook store. Makes sense, nothing special.

Though when Frank leaves, David and I have a good laugh at the coincidence as he takes copies of the book.

Is there a lesson here? Eh, not much of one. Don't meet your heroes? No, I was glad to meet Robert Frank, even if he did draw back from me as if I had leprosy. Fame is fleeting? I don't know, but *The Americans* is still, over sixty years on, as powerful, revolutionary, and simply beautiful as ever.

How about, Always trust my camera, even when it goes haywire, because it knows best?

O.K., that lesson I can't overstate. Trusting my Fuji X100 is the key to everything. I love it, feel as if I'm wedded to it, as if it's a part of me, and then—

* * * * *

THEN I BOUGHT a new camera.

My original one, simply the Fuji X100 (the Like-a Leica, as I like-a to call it), officially came out in September 2010. For the record, it's a fixed-lens, 35mm-equivalent camera with what they call hundreds of thousands of dots. They later came out with S and T models, neither of which seemed to improve much on the original. Maybe some of the weirder, buggier, yes, haywire aspects of the X100 had been fixed, but that was a lot of what I loved about it. It simply did its own crazy shit.

In 2017, Fuji put out the X100F. It seemed to be a major leap forward, and I hadn't bought a new camera in six years, and … it was time.

I took right to it. Don't remember much shake-down cruise, just got out on the street and started snapping. I know my pictures got better, too, not so much image quality as simply better photos, though how much of this was because of the new camera I have no idea. Simply, I'd made a good move.

A few years back I went to my first PhotoPlus show at NYC's Javits Center, fortunately easy to get to with the then fairly new 7 train extension. This was my first visit to a professional photo fair, with manufacturers selling all manner of stuff, and the highest aesthetic seeming to be wedding photos and sunsets over gorges. I felt a little as I did those first trips down to Occupy Wall Street: Everybody was shooting the same thing, but I wanted to shoot everything different.

Still, it was fun at PhotoPlus, and each fall I went back. One year I picked up a Canon Pro-1000 printer at a good discounted price (not quite realizing how expensive ink refills would be; they could've given me the printer for free and still made out like crazy). Another year I got a set of crystals to stick in front of my lens and play around with. Little did I know they'd transform a whole body of my work. (More on this later.)

I found I liked big convention-like fairs, would go each year to the Antiquarian Book Fair on the Upper East Side in hopes of scoring rare photobooks. I've collected vinyl records seriously for twenty-five years. And I had a good time at PhotoPlus, even if I did have to constantly remind myself that I was always after something other than convention.

That's about it from me on camera talk. I don't hear Daido Moriyama talk about his camera; he just talks about going out and taking pictures.

Which leads to a fairly recent photobook of mine. I was watching an hour-long video of Daido out walking around Tokyo snapping away while riffing to the cameraman. It was all in Japanese, of course, with subtitles. One caught my eye, made me freeze the film. It read: "I was just wondering around."

Clearly a mistranslation; they meant "wandering around."

But just as my Fuji X100 cameras kept mistranslating what is in front of me, in the most intriguing and magical ways, so this mistranslation caught everything my photography is about. I took a screenshot, used that photo of mistranslation as a book cover.

I Was Just Wondering Around.

No matter which camera one uses, that says it all.

* * * * *

O.K., SO HOW WAS I doing in coming up with my own vaunted personal voice and vision? You know, those qualities that let me get a little snippy when seeing all the beautiful sunsets at trade shows?

I was starting to get an idea.

The ideal, I knew, was that when you saw a Robert Frank photo (his sneering at me aside) or a Garry Winogrand or a Diane Arbus photo, you simply knew who took it. Could I get anywhere close to that? How *did* I get close to that?

There were no clear lessons, now how-to book. There was, I believed, doing just what I was doing: taking pictures every day, then sorting them into my books; always looking for a new kind of shot, unlike anyone else's; always looking at new work, and yet continuing to dig deep into masterful work; and most of all, keeping my eyes and ears and all my senses as open as possible, those proverbial antennae waving, waiting for tremors and flashes and new angles and new souls with eruptive emotions and always new qualities of light … really, to keep doing what I'd been doing and hope for the best.

Can you yourself tell if you've found a new voice, a new vision? I'm not sure, I think somebody else has to recognize that. You go on what's inside you, what you feel, what comes off right, and wrong, and most of all what sparks excitement. You do the best you can with that, through up days and down. Then somebody else comes along and says, "Look, an original voice, an original vision."

The odd thing? When I've heard words like that from someone I don't quite believe them. It sounds so enormous, so historical. Really, I just do what I do, day in and day out. Indeed, my work simply is me.

I did begin to find new things and places I was drawn to. It seemed I liked big pictures of women's lips, too. O.K., Daido, you got that one. I liked a certain Provoke kind of blur and unfocus, and rather than just let my Fuji simply do what it wanted, I found ways to make the camera get shots like that when I wanted it to; I began to reign in its unruliness, mold its quirks to my own intentions. I also found I liked photos shot through lenses or mirrors, and photos swirled with smoke. (You were wondering when the title of the book, *Mirrors and Smoke*, would turn up, right?)

What I told myself, if nobody else, was that I was trying most of all to capture both our world and also a world coincident with ours, but larger, more mysterious, more spiritual. It's a kind of half-world I've found in the songs and recordings of Bob Dylan, the wonders of Bach, the books of William Blake, the saxophone of John Coltrane, the prose of Herman Melville, the art of El Greco, Edvard Munch, Mark Rothko, and countless others.

Like true perfection or transcendence, to grab and clutch this skittish yet astonishing half-world is impossible, yet all we can strive for.

I still go after that half-world in my writing.

I now go after it in my picture taking, too.

* * * * *

MIRRORS AND SMOKE.

The title of this book, a tad clever I hope. We all know what smoke and mirrors means. I'm hoping my photography is something exactly reversed. Not distraction, obfuscation, or concealment but the opposite: a kind of higher clarity, or understanding, reached through shots into mirrors, around plumes of smoke, into walls that reflect amorphous shapes … into the sun to capture its wide spread of rays.

Simply, I use the words *smoke and mirrors* not to obfuscate but to reveal.

A paradox, but that's what makes it interesting.

*****

SPEAKING OF PARADOXES, or at least unusual juxtapositions, I don't make much of being a novelist who works to be a serious photographer, though I've noted that there are two other novelists in history who have produced notable photobooks, Eudora Welty and Wright Morris, the latter of whom, coincidentally, I studied with briefly in grad school. I bring this up because I recently came across a quote from Jack Kerouac on Robert Frank, about a trip they took to Florida together. Marveling at Frank's ability to drive and at the same time snap away, Kerouac said, "I suddenly realized I was taking a trip with a genuine artist and that he was expressing himself in an art-form that was so unlike my own and yet fraught with a thousand difficulties quite unlike those of my own."

Encouraging words. Frankly, I have to say I find being a photographer vastly simpler and less problematic than being a writer. As I've said above, you get to get away from your desk, and the heavy lift of words from your memory and imagination onto paper; you get to go out and walk in the sun (and occasional rain and sleet); you get to snap away and simply ignore or delete photos that don't work out (you don't have to rewrite them over and over, or toss out whole chapters that get in the way of the story flow, even though they've taken weeks or months to compose); and you can always tell yourself, *They're simply pictures. You know, just a photograph*.

And yet also the work of "a genuine artist."

Photography is interesting that way, it's a little like the rock and roll music I love, just teenage pabulum and noise when a lot of it was brand new, and now worthy of a Nobel Prize. Photography just something that went into papers to wrap dead fish in, or fill up the pages of *Life* and *Look* magazines; and now, well, bedrocks of museums all around the world.

Kerouac makes an interesting case to look at. For all his lifelong writing and life difficulties, we still remember him bennied up and typing away for three weeks to turn out *On the Road* on one long scroll of paper. A myth? Not the scroll; I actually saw it laid out in the rotunda of the main New York Public Library in 2007. The creating a whole book in three weeks, well, as Kerouac's brother-in-law said, "I think what Jack should've said was, 'I typed it up in three weeks.' "

No doubt true, yet also one more fascinating connection between the writer whose intro helped get Grove Press to publish *The Americans* in the first place and the actual practice of photography. Because what else does a photographer do but get an idea or a method or a plan of how their photographs will go (or in my case, often no plan other than to go out wandering and taking pictures), and then execute each photo as quick as can be. Load a single slice of film into your camera for each shot you make? Of course not—you put that film on a roll and let it feed through the camera, and if you're as serious as Garry Winogrand, at least, you get really good at changing film rolls in seconds. Not to mention the "infinite roll of film" the digital flash card in the slot of your Nikon or Leica provides these days.

We plan, we think, we study other photographers, we nail our craft . . . then hyped up on bennies or not, we in effect close our eyes (while keeping them as alive and focused as we can), then type and snap and snap and type till the bloody thing's finished.

And, oh, as for taking photos while I drive, I don't think I'll give it a try, probably more reckless than texting; though I have gotten some fine shots from passenger seats as the world goes whirring and blurring by.

*****

As WILD AND UNBOUND as I am in my art, I admit to keeping my daily life pretty grounded, down to the basic stuff. (No bennies, no drugs for me at all except the occasional glass of wine at dinner.) Especially as I get older. Simple pleasures, a ripe consistency. More Wally Shawn in *My Dinner with Andre* than director Andre Gregory. As long as there's not a dead cockroach in my morning coffee I'm happy, says Wally in paraphrase, explaining why he isn't out gallivanting around the globe as his pal does.

Indeed, I often joke that the secret to my photography on the street is pretty much where I feel like having lunch. My faves, for the record, are Perilla Bulgogi Gobdol or Dol Pan Nakji Dup Bap on W. 32nd Street, and Shanghai noodles or Vietnamese squid in Chinatown south of Canal in Manhattan. When I'm feeling adventurous I take the 7 train out to Queens, either to Jackson Heights for Indian buffet or to the end of the line in Flushing, to our other glorious Chinatown for lamb and squash dumplings.

I only half kid. Day in and day out, in the mornings I write, or work on photos in Lightroom and Photoshop, then put together my books in InDesign … but then it's time to get out in the fresh air, go eat something, head off on long walks, and take pictures.

Of course, from time to time I will stray farther afield for photos (and probably lunch); and if I have to go meet somebody in a part of Brooklyn, say, that I don't know well, I'll have my camera and give myself enough extra time to wander—no, *wonder*—about. I usually don't go out simply to look for photos. It's my faith that good photos are everywhere, at least in New York City (Daido must feel the same about his home, Tokyo), and all I have to do is be tuned in and on the street, with a fresh battery in my Fuji.

I do realize I have it easy-peasy with my one supersmart digital camera, as opposed to those still using film, and developing their own photos. I kind of get what they're probably thinking about me, too. I do collect vinyl records, will argue all day that they sound way better than anything digital. Except that … even if you shoot film, you pretty much have to scan it to digital before you can print it. (Except for the rare wet printing shop.) Since I didn't have any kind of photographic career with my poor man's Nikon those decades back, I don't miss anything, nothing to be nostalgic about. What I do have is my one camera, my essential tool, and I see it as my job to make the most of it on its own terms. In truth, I feel lucky about that. I didn't have to guiltily forgo (or escape) a bunch of time-settled beliefs and rules, I just dug in, figured out my new Fuji as best I could, made the mistakes that turned out to be godsends, then simply tried to get out of its way and let it take the best photos it can.

Well, also the best photos *I* can, since that's where all my energy went: to coming to understand my own vision, my own sensibility, and how to work with my camera to express it for me.

I do have a few moves and feints. One of the best things about the Fuji X100 series is that you can see your focus—the actual photo you're about to take—through the viewfinder. Thus if you're interested in less than perfectly focused shots, you can pretty much see what you'll get. I could also expect the camera to go wiggy on me, too, often in interesting ways (and when not, a couple flicks of my fingertip and … trash that photo). I learned quickly that the photos you remember most are the ones you *did not* take. Indeed, I was just talking to a photographer friend who was planning to drive two hours round trip to go back to snap a photo that she didn't take the first time she went past it. I told her that doing that every once in a while is good for you. It means you won't *not* take the next photo you should, at least for six months. In my experience, every six months you get lazy and choose not to hit your shutter button when you should, then regret it hugely. If spending crazy time going back to try to get a shot you missed keeps you on your toes, and constantly reminds you always to snap away, it's worth it.

I also have no compunction about throwing something in front of the lens. I have a few thises and thats I'll keep close to my (non-film-roll-holding) vest, but I did mention crystals earlier, so let me talk about that. This was a professional set of metal rings that float inches in front of your lens, along with crystals on sticks to attach to the rings. The exhibit at PhotoPlus had lots of dreamy advertising shots taken through their two crystal sets. I wasn't interested in any of that, but I'm always up to try something different, so I picked up Crystal Pack No. 2.

It had a set of long, narrow manmade crystals. I found one in particular, stuck it in front of my lens, did strange and compelling things. Not long after I got it, something happened and the stick broke off; all I had was the crystal itself, sharp glass bottom and all. In the way of things, the broken-off crystal worked better for my purposes than the official mounted one. I wrapped some duct tape around the end so I couldn't cut myself and twisted it tight. Then I started wandering.

The cover of my book *War Horse* is through the crystal, as are many other shots in that book, though not all. In the city the crystal was like a certain brush I could use; I had others.

Then the pandemic swept in and we ended up in Woodstock, New York. The country. Nature, everywhere.

A problem: I wanted to keep taking photos, needed to take photos almost every day. But I had no interest in taking nature photos. I couldn't see anything about nature shots that hadn't been done, by people who really knew what they were doing. And I couldn't see how my shooting a picture of a flower or a tree would get my vision any closer to that half-world I'm always trying to slip my photos into.

Enter the broken-off crystal. I quickly discovered that by simply sticking it in front of the lens as I stayed close to home, I could get the images I wanted from trees, bushes, water, sky. Not nature as it was but as it could be, as only I and the camera saw it.

Simple as that.

* * * * *

THE CRYSTAL ISN'T A GIMMICK, though, or a trick or game I play with the world. It's simply a tool I use to make the world reveal itself in new ways, with new truths.

What's great about twisting this shard of glass before my lens is that each minute turn changes everything, colors, shades, images, streaks of light. The most minute flick.

Which is one thing I love about photography, how there is no level of detail too infinitesimal to affect a photograph. As discussed before, a millisecond here or there can make or unmake a photo. A flicker or splatter of light, or even a wrinkle in a bath of light, can also make a photo. If getting mastery over any art is in controlling every detail as much as possible (while leaving yourself open to mysterious and magical happenstance), in some ways to reach this control with photography (since you're not creating out of nothing, as in filling a blank screen with words, a blank canvas with paint) is to become a master of actual time and space.

Wait, did he actually say that? Becoming a photographer has made him a master of time and space? Isn't that a little … grand?

Too grand? Sure, probably. I do feel funny just having written the previous paragraph, and can't tell yet whether I want to proclaim it too loudly, though it sure feels true. All you're doing is taking pictures of the world as it is before your lens, even if there's some manipulation involved. And what is the world but time and space, light and dark (and color, glorious color), and life and death?

The building blocks of all art, but with photography you don't conjure them in your head or at a piano or in a studio, you have to go out and wrench them all directly from the world itself. Why wouldn't that be a form of mastery?

* * * * *

O.K., BACK DOWN TO EARTH. Or, worse, an earth not much familiar at all.

The first draft of this book was written holed up in Woodstock during the heart of the pandemic, when I shot nature through my crystal, turning the world we thought we knew into landscapes as deeply unrecognizable as the actual world had become deeply unrecognizable.

This is hardly the first time I've launched into a new kind of photographic series. For better or worse, I shoot in a lot of different ways. There are the chiaroscuro surprise street portraits of my *Human Kindness Overwhelming* books. Then there's the painterly expressionism of *All That Is Solid Melts into Air*. (For both these series, I perched myself in specific places in midtown Manhattan, for one standing inside a glass bus stop shooting at a forest-green construction wall on Fifth Avenue, for the other shooting into the surfaces of a deep doorway on West 45th Street right off Times Square.)

Early on I found I had a thing for Halloween, though I wasn't interested simply in people in costumes; that had been done delightfully by Helen Levitt and devilishly by Ralph Eugene Meatyard. What I wanted were photos closer to capturing that half-light life that always fascinates me. I found what I wanted in Union Square in the city on October 31, the place where post–Village Halloween Parade souls wash up. I followed my usual rules of street photography—get close, no closer; and play with focus, and light and shadow—and got a series of shots of mystery and magic that went into the book *A Carnival of Souls*, and when I have enough new Halloween photos, its follow-up, *Danse Macabre*. The goal was to not shoot people in costumes but something wholly other, and also to …

… Spin on a dime.

That is, I've done a number of photobooks that came about on the spot, due to the circumstances I was in. I might have even gone in with an expectation of what I'd be shooting (as with Halloween in New York City), but would have to quickly recalculate as I tried to grok in fullness the essence of what was going on right then and there.

A good case in point is my book *Shibuya Time*. Another October 31 night, this time in Tokyo. I'd been in Kyoto, shooting away, but since it was Halloween, and since it only comes once a year (duh), I took a train that morning back to the capital, ready to go shoot as many photos as I could. I was worried that Halloween would be no big deal in Japan, and … how wrong I was. Not just one night but a week of festivities. Not just one part of town but all over. A bit of online research and I decided to head out to Shibuya, which when I got there … wow!

Shibuya in all my previous visits had left me turned about and mostly lost, and this night was that to excess. Every street was brimful of costumed kids. I immediately plunged in, intending to take the kind of mysterious and otherworldly Halloween shots I was used to from New York City. I quickly realized, Nope, that won't work; what I was in the middle of was in no way the same kind of celebration. Halloween in Japan was evidently a fairly recent import, and the teenagers and twentysomethings reveling in it had only progressed so far in costumes, lots of tawdry makeup, some catty clothes, a lot of jokey police uniforms, and more cleavage than you'd probably see any other day of the year in Tokyo. But there sure were a lot of people, some streets so compressed with bodies I couldn't walk in any kind of line but simply got pressed along in this quivering amoeba form as it oozed down the street.

I started snapping. I got close—due to the squeeze of bodies, I simply *was* close—and looked more for emotions and angles and strong photos than anything other-worldly or transcendent. I snapped away. I was getting good shots. Any concern that I wasn't in the right place for Halloween quickly disappeared, and that was before I met an English photographer who told me he flew to Japan every year for the whole Halloween week, that there was nothing like it anywhere. "The largest Halloween celebration in the world," he told me.

Could be. Not haunted bone-deep as the Eastern U.S. is by Nathaniel Hawthorne and Washington Irving and Salem witch trials, or everywhere in America by 1970s horror flicks such as *Texas Chain Saw Massacre*, *Dawn of the Dead*, and John Carpenter's celebrated original *Halloween*; instead Tokyo was shallow yet fresh, and revolutionary: This tight-bound society letting its youth go wild for a night.

So that was my book *Shibuya Time*. Not at all what I intended going in to shoot, but what I found ... and all the more exciting to me because of that.

Indeed, I'm always happy when the ideas I have going in quickly die. So much of the delight of photography is in the discovery, trying to suss out those essences and figure out how to shoot them. I did another book from that Japan trip in 2018, *Lost in Tokyo*. They're not simply shots of Tokyo but everywhere I was in Japan, especially Kyoto. My approach was my usual: Hang my camera in its case over my shoulder and go out wandering ... O.K., in Daido's home especially, go out wondering. See what I'd see. Snap what I could. Reflexes fast, eyes always moving. Not really that different from what I do all the time back home in New York City, just that I was halfway around the world, and—

Lost.

Well, not all the time (I did ride the subway regularly in Tokyo, and only missed a stop once), and all the while getting dozens and dozens of strong photos. It's just that I didn't even begin to understand Japan. I did the best I could, but at bottom I simply wanted to get around, see as much as I could, buy some classic photobooks, eat some sushi, then find my way back to my hotel at night. If anybody asks how much I understood of the nation I was visiting for the first time, I hold up a thumb and pointer finger merely a few hairs apart.

And yet I made a very strong book. Because as in all my books they're not solely about where *I* am, they're about me and my camera being where I am.

A subtle difference, perhaps just the difference between a documentary photographer, out to bring home the news of where they are for all to see, and the kind of photographer I work to be, in which it's my eye and imagination that colors what I shoot, what goes into one of my photobooks.

That is, although I've made books of many different places and subjects, they all come from me … they're all mine, my vision, my will, my eye, my magic Fuji.

Shibuya Time was a one-night book. I've made other books that are also simply circumscribed periods of time in one place. One afternoon my wife and I were let in to the modernist sculptor Raoul Hague's old home not far from us in the Maverick Colony in Woodstock. Hague lived primitively, with electricity but still getting water from a hand pump, spending all his time carving his powerful large wood sculptures. When he died in 1993 at age 88 his house became the center of his foundation.

We were there for about an hour or so. As Pat discussed upkeep with the caretaker, I went around snapping photos. As always, I tried to shoot what nobody else had or would. I was encouraged by being part of a vivid tradition. Robert Frank had shot photos at Hague's house, and Lee Friedlander had done a whole book there (*Witness #6*).

I discovered little found sculptures on shelves that were probably just the way Hague had left them, curious wall hangings, his outdoor wood stove and rusted water pump, even patterns of paint on the walls. I titled the collection after a phrase of Hague's, *It Talks, It Whispers*. That's what the house did for me that August day in 2017, and that's what I strove to photograph: the way the home itself talked and whispered.

Another brief project and a book I have a special feeling for is *Spirit Test*. This came from a couple visits to a Warhol show at the Whitney museum in winter-spring 2018–19. One room there was dedicated to Warhol's short *Screen Test* films, which consisted of nothing more than one of his Factory mates sitting in a chair for four or so minutes, the length it took for one of his 100-foot rolls of film to spool through his 16mm Bolex, then slowed down for exhibition.

This was an ongoing part of the Warhol show, just a dark room with some chairs and eight or so films on continuous loop. I took a seat, watched awhile, then lifted my camera, opened the shutter, and waved the Fuji about as it faced the screen.

Yes, waved the camera, snapshots from a quick flourish left to right.

What would I capture? I had no idea. Except that what I saw on playback was enigmatic, fascinating … traces of the person on the black screen, blurred, streaked … spirit-like.

I kept waving my camera at the screen, took a dozen or so snaps. They looked good at the museum, back home they looked even better. I quickly came up with the title of the book, the punful *Spirit Test*, and decided to go back one more time to get enough photos to fill it out. When I had enough, I used Lightroom to colorize the shots, then worked up the best order and made the book.

The above titles are some of the specifically focused, one- or two-day books I've done. There are other single-focus books, too. A group of self-portraits in which I like to think I'm not truly recognizable in any photo: *Eye and Eye*, another word play, this time on the Reggae phrase (and Dylan song) *I and I*. There's *Flags*, which is just that, pictures of flags both actual and figurative. (Me getting my Jasper Johns on.) There's *Meeting Robert Frank*, as discussed above.

But most of my books are in essence culled from the flood of city photos I've taken, poured into Lightroom, then sorted out as ideas and titles came to me. For me the title is always a hugely important part of the book. When I first got going I made those two one-off books with Blurb just to see what was what: *Demons and Dogs*, and *Razzle Dazzle* ... books that hold up, yet show me finding the full breadth of my art.

Along the way there's been *I Shall Be Free #7* (extra points for those who know where that title comes from), *Purloined Souls*, *Electrick Spirits*, and everybody's favorite title, *Taylor Swift Doesn't Own the Color Red*, the latter all photos in which red predominates.

As in, color is always central to my work, wild splashes of it, Impressionism bubbling over into Expressionism, rich hues (and emotions) abounding. If serious black and white photography is in essence the play of light and shadow, my photography is the play of bright and somber colors, clashes and harmonies of tones, and essences of light and shadow, but in color. (I admit Alex Webb is the master of this kind of shooting, and it's true he has far more patience than I have. Though as the title of this book attests, I'm more intrigued by obfuscation and mystery than in crisp colors in intense floods of light.)

It's also true that vivid and provocative bursts of color are not all I'm interested in. I have those two books entitled *Human Kindness Overwhelming*, one *Spring* and the other *Winter*, that feature an intense chiaroscuro; photos, all of people walking past me on the street, in which only slices of their faces and/or parts of their bodies are visible.

I can't remember exactly the moment I stumbled on this way of shooting, just where I was. For some reason I stopped at a bus stop on Fifth Avenue near 52nd Street, around the corner from the Museum of Modern Art. Across the sidewalk from the glass enclosure a building was being erected. (It turned out to be Nike's flagship store.) In front of the building site was a dark-green painted wood construction wall, and I found that if I pressed up against the glass of the back of the covered bus stop, then did this and that with my Fuji, with a certain kind of off-focus and twists of my free hand, I could get these chiaroscuro shots of people walking past.

They were startling and powerful.

That bus stop at 52nd and Fifth wasn't the only spot in the city I'd return to again and again looking for photos. Sometimes I'd go old-school and, paying homage to great photographers fiftysome years earlier such as Winogrand and Meyerowitz, I'd hover at Fifth and 42nd, by the main NY Public Library, and hope to get a good street shot. And sometimes I did, but most of the time I found I'd just be taking photos that, well, had been done far better all those years ago.

I had other places I'd end up fairly regularly, mostly building surfaces from which I could catch the kind of reflected shot I fancied. Mirrors that were anything but actual mirrors.

And I kept going back to that covered bus stop in front of the being-erected Nike flagship store, taking pictures, both winter and summer, until I had enough photos for the two volumes of *Human Kindness Overwhelming*.

Then the building wall went down and the Nike store opened. To assuage my disappointment, I went into the store and found that if I sat in the far corner on the ground floor and did some more this and that with my Fuji, I could get a whole other kind of interesting shot through the bands of translucent white on the large plate-glass window. One of these shots graces the cover of this book, three shadowed businessmen before the burst of a yellow cab, apparent clouds of white smoke shaping and obscuring them.

And, full disclosure, I missed the building being built at Fifth Avenue and 52nd Street so much that I later found one going up near Fifth Avenue and 32nd, around the corner from my fave Korean lunch joint, with another covered bus stop with glass, from which, with another twist of this and that with my Fuji, I could get a whole other flavor of chiaroscuro faces and bodies as they walked by. This was deep in the pandemic; the resulting book: *Masks*.

Further books have come from places I've traveled, *Shibuya Time* and *Lost in Tokyo*, as discussed above, followed by *Star of Light*, from my subsequent hop over to Bangkok. A year later I was in Italy; *Prego!* came from that trip. That's always a cheery challenge: not just to be on vacation, but to try to sip the essence of where I am, darting and intense, like a hummingbird pulling nectar from a flower, and turn it into a photobook.

Mostly, of course, I'm home in New York City, and from there many more photobooks have come: *The Lord Mocks the Mockers*, *He Do the Police in Different Voices*, *Black Cat Bone*, *War Horse*, *Frog*, and *Chain of Fools*. (Hey, maybe one day I'll turn all my book titles into a poem.) The first title here is from the photo on that book's cover, a sign on another green construction wall on Fifth Avenue with a fluttery pigeon rising above it. The next comes from T.S. Eliot, his early title for *The Waste Land*, a hugely influential work for me. *Black Cat Bone* comes from a lyric from country blues tunes from the 1930s, further grand influences. *War Horse* just seemed to fit the splintered purple photo of smiling faces looming over a statue of a horse, oddly dropped in the center of Times Square. *Frog* … no real explanation, just sounded right. And *Chain of Fools* because the cover photo is of a series scarlet-shoed bridesmaids, legs out in Williamsburg, Brooklyn, and the final shot is of me and my good photographer friend Fred Cray, the guy who runs around secreting one-off prints of his photos in books in stores and museums, and who has a large following of his own.

Then, as mentioned above, the pandemic hit, and taking city photos became impossible.

I did a trilogy of books of my fractured upstate nature shots, *Bad Moon/Code Sun*, *Surf City*, and *Ragged and Dirty*, all packaged together working with my studio manager, Bruno Jansen, in a homemade box under the title *Woodstock 2020*. Then it was back to the city, and back to wondering about, leading to a companion trilogy, *New York 2021*, comprised of *Shuttertown*, *Cool Struttin'*, and *Naked* (the latter inspired by a shot I took of a Hispanic man sitting on West 46th Street polishing the boots of the famous Naked Cowboy of Times Square).

I keep on making books. To capture the tail end of the worst of the pandemic, I made *La Mala Hora (Evil Hour)*, then to celebrate the hope of an abundant postpandemic world, I made *Lush*. Bruno and I cooked up another trilogy, which we call *Three Modal Photobooks*—each book modeled after its predominant color. The books are the already mentioned *Taylor Swift Doesn't Own the Color Red*, grouped with the new collections *The Sun's Not Yellow, It's Chicken* and *Kind of Blue*; a photobook series built not on traditional chords and rhythms but constructed upon unusual harmonies and tonalities. (Yep, I love all kinds of music; and always see my photobooks in musical terms. Indeed, I suggest my students edit their own books to a loud-playing soundtrack of the tunes that undergird their own books. As in, put on Howlin' Wolf and get a dark, bluesy feel, Bob Marley and rise to his complex joy, or Beyoncé and just dance those photos into place.)

I also always want to try something new. For better or worse, I shoot in a lot of different ways. Recently I moved on to something wholly different. On my first-ever trip to the Florida Keys I had the notion to do a composite book; to take the best wondering-about shots I could, but also photos of the abundantly colorful flowers, and (from a tip from a friend while I was down there) butterflies, from the magical Butterfly Conservatory, then layer them all together in composite prints. The book that came out, *Searching for Infinity*, is one of my strongest.

Also innovative and powerful is *Red Balloon*, crystal shots of the lantern-ball-festooned streets of Manhattan's Chinatown. (A good reason to head down there: the Singapore Chow Mei Fun at H.K. Wonton Garden, topped by the best hot chili oil I've found.) In the first copies of *Red Balloon*, Bruno and I dropped a nonphotographic surprise. A hint: We're hoping that in fifty years, unlike Warhol's book *Index*, our surprise hasn't melted into the pages.

More New York City books in the works as I type this: *It's Violet*, *The Ghost Time* (all of the books photos taken from the back of a bus on March 15, 2022, on a trip up and back to Harlem, and lunch at the great Charles' Pan Fried Chicken on W. 145th St.), *Salt Peanuts*, and *We Are Not OK*. The latter book was inspired by black sheets with cut-out letters reading WE ARE NOT OK that activists pasted over a neon-ad screen in Times Square, where I ended up after chasing Manhattanhenge from the back of, yep, another bus. That work of public art/protest followed one more mass shooting in America; and so does my book.

So what next? What will future books be?

Well, I'm piling up photos for a few projects, with as yet no end in sight. One will be called *From the Back of the Bus*, because, you got it, I've been riding a lot of city buses lately. (Besides *The Ghost Time*, another bus book, *Swing Street*, is already out.) I'll keep doing that, and I'll also keep taking crystal shots of NYC for a book I'm calling *Unreal City*. I love these kinds of ongoing projects, for which I can shoot wherever I am, whatever I'm doing. It keeps me busy and with a degree of personal agency if the flow of good photos on the street is running dry that day.

And then who knows?

As I've written here, and always say, that's the essential nature of photography: You don't make it up at a desk (or, for me, in a studio), you have to be right there where the photo is being shot.

So that's my faith. That future books will come from new ideas spawned in the moment depending on where I am, what's in front of me, and what new and interesting ways I can see the world around. That's the adventure, the delight: There's no way to know now what future work will be. As with most of my photographs, they will be born in the moment, no matter where a new idea ultimately leads.

And that's what I always love about being a photographer: I truly do not know what I'll be shooting tomorrow. It depends on where I am (O.K., and what's for lunch), what I see there, and the ways my Fuji ends up pushing me beyond my intentions.

Endless surprise!

* * * * *

PEOPLE OFTEN SAY TO ME (indeed, you're probably thinking right now): You sure make a lot of photobooks. What's up with that?

I get it, sometimes it can feel odd even to me, as if I'm churning out too much work. Yet I believe all of my photobooks are as strong and tightly edited as they can be, and all are singular expressions. So what gives?

For one, I take a lot of photos. As I've said above, I'm always out with my camera, and always hawk-eyed for photos to snap. I also like to keep busy, need to do work each day. It's part of the calling of being a photographer, close to the basis of the work, its essence.

When I was first getting going as a novelist John Irving told me about his daily practice. He said that he had to do something each day to "redeem the day"—to make it a day worth living, to quiet regrets. For him (and for me back then) it was doing a good day's work at the typewriter.

Irving went on to say that if the work had gone poorly or unproductively, he could redeem the day by making a good meal … but it had to be something. Hard, intense work in hopes of blessing each day, sanctifying it, or at least sealing off the always present existential dread .

Then there's Bernard Malamud. I worked for him in the final years of his life. He's the writer about whom Philip Roth, as he set down to his own long, monkish days at the typewriter, always said to himself: "Malamud has already been at it for two hours."

That was the serious novelist's task: long days, every day, at the typewriter or computer, that always lonely lift into blankness, with mere words as stepping stones. Lost to the work. In your core needing to do the work.

Turns out I bring that same need to my photo taking. A day with one good photo can redeem it; and more good photos that day are only further blessings. And hard, driven work is the whole deal.

So I keep snapping away.

I also love to make photobooks, it's so joyful and fun after the steep, near-impossible push of writing novels, and I revel in it. Hence, a lot of photobooks get made.

Then there's Ari Maricopolous. Not my very favorite photographer, but certainly a productive one and in one way an inspiration.

When I was just getting going with my own work Maricopolous was in the middle of a project with Dashwood Books called *Anyway*. The idea was to put out a new zinelike volume each week. Yep, a new book, every single week. Books most often full of free-associating street shots or photos lightly autobiographical. Some books are themed, by colors or subject. Others simply hang together. A lot of sidewalks, a lot of graffiti, a lot of friends, even a few girlie magazines. And each one works on its own terms, with its own strengths.

A book a week. No time to stop, probably not much time to think … and the work all the better for it. A full year, at the end of which Maricopolous had fifty-two books, all collected in a nice cardboard box.

I loved the idea of this project, wished I had a similar task. So not only did I subscribe to the *Anyway* series, but in my own way I set out to do something similar. Thus my series of *Angel Parade* books, and then all the other ones I've made.

Too many of them? I certainly don't think so.

For me they're simply enough.

* * * * *

EARLIER I WROTE THAT the photos you remember most are the ones you didn't take. That's certainly true, but I'm also fascinated by how well I remember the circumstances of almost every good photo I've taken. Place, time of day, even more specific aspects in fine detail. I look at them, and I'm right back there with something catching my eye, getting that frisson of *Hmmn, could make a good photo*, and snapping the shutter.

Here's how I account for that. As the world around us is a constant flow of time and space, and photographs are a memorializing of discreet moments of that deep, ever-present flow, then my recollection of taking the picture is tied directly to why I took the picture in the first place. Think of it this way. There are moments we'll always remember, historical events so profound that where we were and what we were doing are stamped in memory. For someone of my age, JFK being assassinated. (I heard about it on my school playground.) The Beatles on *Ed Sullivan*. (In front of the wood-console TV, after eager anticipation all day—and I wasn't even a true Beatles fan then.) September 11th. (Working on a novel at home, looking out at a beautiful cyan sky, looking forward to heading downtown to buy the Dylan album *Love and Theft*, released on that day—then hearing the first reports on the radio.) Historical moments that forever rupture the parade of our days.

I'm thinking of my photos as small, personal versions of the way a common day can be jolted so memorably. As if the vast quotidian scrim of what we all pass through half-knowingly is suddenly pierced by a presence more urgent, grand, possibly beautiful or deeply meaningful … or at least damn interesting. Yes a scrim, let's call it a thin beige cloth we can only partially see through, that enwrapping ordinariness that surrounds every part of our lives … punched, torn by the unexpected, the special … an eruption that can challenge and change everything.

It's these tears in the scrim, when the deeper, truer world pops through, that I search for with my camera, and hope to catch.

And always remember.

That's the truly odd and powerful thing: It's as if the world is presenting me (us?) with a force of memory that exists before it is recognized, let alone remembered. Sending out intimations that say the next seconds will be worth capturing in a photo. Telling us to be ready. Fling out that camera. Snap that shutter. Grab the moment for all you're worth.

These notions are tied in with much of what I've already said about the nature of an important photograph, that it's the manifestation of that which demands our attention, and jolts our consciousnesses even before we know it.

I'm talking about this again because it's the only way I can explain why I can remember so well when and where I took a photograph while the rest of my life more and more simply blurs itself along.

And why I hope the photos that I remember taking are memorable to everyone reading this, too.

*****

I'VE BEEN THINKING ABOUT the simple miracle of my Fuji. I was out taking pictures, nothing special, actually I was picking up bread from the local bakery, walking the dog, looking for something to shoot. I pull my camera out of my bag, flick the switch on, and … it works.

Of course it works, you numskull, you think. Well, yeah. It does. Every time I turn it on, it's ready to go. Well, almost every time. There was that weird moment when I was meeting Robert Frank for the first time and it shifted over to movie mode. There have been other times, actually quite a few, when the camera has a mind of its own. And as I've written, I welcome that. I know a lot of what I do is a collaboration between my ideas and the camera's own ideas.

But this is a simple paean to how well-made and efficient the Fuji is. As in, it's there when I need it, and I don't have to worry otherwise.

Which is no small thing.

As I get older, having things that work is far more important than it seemed to be years ago. Maybe things just didn't work that well those years back, before computers and robots made sure parts fit, well-tuned software harmonized things, and the whole deal functioned smoothly. Or maybe it was that *I* didn't work that well, and couldn't expect that much more from the things I owned and utilized.

I certainly expect myself to work well now, especially when I'm out in the streets with my camera. I expect to take that deep breath and put myself into my photo-taking head. I expect to be quick of sight, and as fast as possible with hitting the shutter when a possible photo pops up. I even like to think I'm in training when I play a game on my iPhone in which you have to line up shiny balls so they match into lines, then explode. My wife calls it "the bad game," as in, "you're wasting time"; but I like to think of it as a way to keep eye-hand–shutter finger coordination sharp.

Which is all important, especially when out walking about. There's so much to take in, and barely milliseconds to decide that a flickering moment in front of me might make a strong photo.

All my parts have to work well, and of course so does my camera.

So, again, dear ol' Fuji X100, I have nothing but affection and love. You're my favorite bat, the only one I believe I can hit home runs with. You're my Fender Strat, pre-CBS, which has a tone nothing since could replicate. You're the only knife I dare take to that summer squash sitting there on the kitchen table.

And yet you're so much more. I certainly hope my Wüsthof knife doesn't suddenly develop a mind of its own and start carving the way it wants to go. I hope my guitar doesn't start playing "Louie Louie" while I'm in the middle of "Up on Cripple Creek."

But when that Fuji tells me that it wants the photo to look like this, not that; when it decides on its own focal point; when it blurs out in a way that makes what I'm shooting so much more interesting than the subject at hand; when it splinters the sunlight in a way that makes the whole picture glow in ecstasy … well, I offer up my simple thanks.

High-precision machine and soulful artist. No wonder I'm not interested in any other cameras or lenses or any of that PhotoPlus kind of stuff.

*****

JUST AS MY CAMERA often surprises me, I often surprise myself. That's another thing I love about photography. I'll be out walking around with my camera, mostly just going about my business, doing this or that, and something inside of me bubbles up and says, *Take a picture … now*.

The best is when I have no expectation for what's grabbed me. And in one way best of all are those wall or building surfaces I can shoot into to get the warp and coloring and pattern for the kind of photos I like (those mirrors and smoke); that is, a place I can return to that will always yield interesting shots, where the place creates a uniform frame or look but the people walking past, as different and vast as humanity, change. These are places I can stand for a good while, doing what Walt Whitman did: "loafe and invite my soul."

In truth, I welcome everyone's souls to my camera lens.

I have one of these special places on West 32nd Street, near my fave Korean lunch joints. Then there's Times Square. Friends from out of town say, "You're a real New Yorker, right? I hear real New Yorkers never go to Times Square."

"Not me," I answer. "I go there all the time. I love Times Square."

Why? Because that's where those souls, as different and vast as humanity, are to be found. Packed in tight to Times Square.

Tourists may walk around New York like tourists, stopping in the middle of the sidewalk as if they're in a mall back in Kansas, or clogging street corners as if they're in Chengdu, but they're also all so different. Native garb, intriguing hair styles, and all those faces … those different faces.

Also, more building faces that suit my aesthetic. One is a mirror-surface in a clothing emporium on Broadway near West 45th. Then there's my most significant, on West 46th Street, off of Broadway.

This is the doorway to a building that houses a number of rehearsal studios and acting classes. I've been standing there trying to discreetly take my snaps as students come and go discussing the finer points of *King Lear*. The vestibule is about seven feet wide and ten feet long, from sidewalk to door. It's a kind of green marble. I quickly found that if I focus my camera on a bright light across the street and shoot tight into the marble, the most interesting painterly photos result. You'd never know it from the shots, but a lot depends on what kind of delivery truck is parked by the nearest curb. (Indeed, I just double-checked the location on Google Street View, and my vestibule is blocked by a large brown UPS truck, a reflection of the Google camera car right where I'd be snapping away.)

My photos also depend on what time of day or night it is, and how many people are walking by. It's best as a nighttime perch, since the photos I'm after are all about the streaks and swirls of color; and of course the light-puffs and shadows of the people I'm capturing. Friday and Saturday nights are best, theater traffic, or just tourists heading to Times Square. The slower people move—yep, tourists agape at the Crossroads of the World—the better. If a group of people stop in front of where my camera is pointing, that's always great. As they pause and gab, I have time to try this, try that, and usually get something special.

As with all these photos that are not simply figurative shots of people on the street, that is, the more abstract ones, the ones where the Fuji really works its magic, I don't actually know what I have till I get home and throw them all into Lightroom, perhaps weeks later.

So I just keep snapping. And that's somewhere else intuition comes in strongly. I'll head over to my West 46th Street vestibule when I'm in the area, when I've been out wondering about for hours and when I'm not sure where else to go. And I'll stay there for as a long as … well, as long as I do.

That is, I always try to listen to myself, or my muse; or maybe I'm just paying attention to when I get a bit flagged. Because … O.K., that's it. Time to go. Hardly an intuition, barely a thought, just that it's time to go.

Off to the 1 train at 50th Street and Broadway, maybe a few more snaps along the way, and then it's the subway uptown and home.

I've taken more than five hundred of these West 46th Street photos over the last few years, and I've sorted them down into a book. But I haven't put it out yet. I've been uncertain of a title. I've gone from *Street Strut* to the current one, *All That Is Solid Melts into Air*, since that's what the photos do, turn regular souls on the street into swirls and mists of light and air.

Pure visual essence.

*****

I'VE TALKED A LOT SO FAR about taking photos on the street, and all the qualities you need—imagination; speed; fearlessness (I've learned a few things about that over the years); and simply a good eye—but I haven't mentioned yet how you also need to feel the street's rhythm, its pulse, in your eyes, in your bones.

Which means we need to talk about photography and music again.

As I've said, I love all kinds of music, from Bach to the Beatles, from Muddy Waters to John Coltrane, from Bruce Springsteen to Haim. I get a lot of my inspiration for photographs from listening to music; and more, the music gives me a place to go to calm myself or stimulate myself, to get grounded and always, always find inspiration.

Inspiration? Interesting word, and what does it mean? The row of greeting cards at the shop under the sign INSPIRATIONAL? The wind that comes along now and then and moves you in a certain direction? That first shaft of sunlight through a morning window that somehow gets you out of bed?

Maybe. But how about a ripe and breath-stealing charge that steals upon you, electrifying body and soul, then setting both off together on their appointed tasks?

Simply the spark that inflames the work we're here on this earth to do.

Bob Dylan on Robert Johnson: "From the first note the vibrations from the loudspeaker made my hair stand up. The stabbing sounds from the guitar could almost break a window.... I immediately differentiated between him and anyone else I had ever heard."

Isn't that the thing? We want our hair to stand up! Like the cover of the first *Zap* comix back in the day, Flakey Foont plugged into the wall and nearly exploding.

I've looked at photographs that do that, blow the top of my head off, as well as open up a world I hardly knew existed but that immediately felt more essential and necessary than the world around me. Photos, as well as music, that speak directly to me, that take me somewhere original and more powerful, more electric than anything else ... photos that at bottom inspire me to take my own photos that will also take me to this special place.

Here's another rock icon on the same music Dylan's talking about: "I listen to a lot of country blues still. It still hits me as being the essence of things, somehow, and I can't quite put my finger on it." That's Keith Richards of the Stones.

And that's what I feel when I listen to Johnson or Son House or Howlin' Wolf, mysterious barely graspable truths that tug me down to that good ol' essence of things, records of such power they can fuel a whole life's work, all in the plaintive cry of a slide guitar, the tortured (or triumphantly joyous) wail of a voice. That's the marvel of the blues. You're standing on a street corner, that guy next to you? The devil Himself. That crow strutting past? His spirit embodied. Everywhere you turn: mystery and truth. A woman with a sultry smile who'll drive you blind; a dollar dancing before you that'll break your heart; that promise of water, you drink it down, it ain't nothing but gasoline.

A strange world of mystery and hoodoo. And always there to tap into.

That's what we want from our inspirations, isn't it? We want grounding. We want fuel (water when we're thirsty, gasoline when we gotta roll). We want simplicity and coherence. And we want it there whenever we need it.

And sometimes complexity of the highest order, so our imaginations lift and sweep and corkscrew in ways that expand our own possibilities. That's when I go to Bach's "Goldberg variations" or his solo violin sonatas and partitas, or even more, his solo cello suites, performed by Janos Starker. That's when I go to the Beethoven Violin Concerto. That's when I go to John Coltrane, especially his Impulse records. Or Miles Davis and *Bitches Brew*. Ornette Coleman and *Free Jazz*. And dozens of other complex pieces.

Listening to them you hear an abundance of melodic and harmonic lines. I love playing a good vinyl record on my stereo so I can hear as much richness and complexity as the music holds, and follow it all clearly. All those instruments. All those note patterns. All those complex interactions. Something I'll be talking about next, synesthesia, violins and cellos and horns and glockenspiels erupting as colors; and you watch them as you would an orchestra or a simple blues band, colors that blend and move about and flash and go quiet as in a great painting, or as in a great photograph.

Great music both simple and pure yet elaborate and complex. Always emotional. Always mind-blowing. And at its best, always working to elaborate a vivid complexity yet reveal the simplest of truths.

And that's when I go back to Bob Dylan.

In my book *Mysteries of Light*, I talk about Dylan as a kind of photobook maker, and I focus particularly on "Desolation Row," its opening verse, if I may quote myself, "with its flow of vivid pictures: postcards of hangings, brown passports, beauty parlors swelling with sailors, a circus new in town … and that's just the first four lines of the eleven-minute song."

Bob Dylan always fires up streams of images in my mind. Sometimes I listen to him at four a.m. when I can't sleep, and then return to bed with my own flow of coruscating words igniting my mind. One line after another, one image, one delight, one truth.

Again, how far are lyrics like these from a great photobook?

I'm talking about songwriters here rather than poets because, even as poetic a songwriter as Dylan still has to put a four-four behind his words. That's also what a great photobook artist does: lays down a beat, a rhythm, behind the pictures.

These artists who most inspire me, though, do something else. They get me into this liminal space between our world and other worlds that I'm often seeking in my own work. In a word, they transcend.

Blurs and streaks, mirrors and smoke. Eruptions of color. The eternal mystery of just what's before us, and what's not. The way a great photograph is both here and not here, known and unknown, its imagery hovering right at a wavering border of the known world and other worlds beyond.

Simply, that Alice Quinn lesson from pages and pages back: Seeing what's before me, and what's not. The front, the back, and everything else implied and luminous … all that makes our hair stand on end … and seeing all of it at the same time.

*****

READING OVER THE PREVIOUS SECTION, I see I'm hinting at an occult realm when I say things like "what's before us, and what's not," and "imagery hovering right at a wavering border of the known world and other worlds beyond."

But I'm not. That's the beauty of photography. If there are photographs out there that purport to show ghosts or spirits, well, all they really show us is what the camera lens saw, which means somebody probably had a lot of charlatan kicks with light or double exposures or Photoshop. Duane Michals sure had fun with stuff like this.

I'm never trying to show you anything that's not there. I'm simply making pictures. And when I talk about images along the borders of one world or another, I'm simply after *images* … I'm after vision and art.

I'm also after that synesthesia I mentioned above. Another of my favorite words. *Synesthesia* basically means that one form of sensation gets mixed up with another. That you hear colors, see sounds, feel light, smell whole worlds not visible or apparent, reach out and embrace modalities beyond logic or even possibility….

O.K., I'm getting a little carried away with my definition, but you get the idea. For me, synesthesia gets at what I want all my photos to do: put as much of the world into them as possible, all kinds of senses beyond just the visual, this world and that world, and mix it all up.

Here's another way to think about it.

The first novel I wrote was called *Negative Space*. I finished it in the late 1970s, and it was under contract to a major publisher (no longer extant) until it was bumped for budgetary reasons, a cut that still stings.

I mention *Negative Space* now because the title still intrigues me. The thing is, I haven't looked at the manuscript to the book in decades, and can barely remember much about it. But I do know that the concept of negative space presents a mystery in the book the characters have to solve, and that it involves a loss in the American spirit—a once positive force that has doubled back on itself, and lost its purpose and strength.

You've probably heard of negative space in photography. We're told it's the empty space around a subject that helps give that subject definition. Fair enough … and most likely a useful concept for the budding photographer to grasp.

So why am I still fascinated by the whole idea of negative space? Because for me it ties in with my fascination with synesthesia, that the best photographs aren't only of what's there, what we see, but also of what we don't see; that there's another realm of time and space behind them. I want my photos to probe those borders, to mix up positive and negative just as synesthesia mixes up physical senses; to make a photograph empty itself out even as it abounds in fullness.

It's simply putting everything there is in the world into a photograph. Along with everything that is *not* in the world. Or everything that perhaps could be there but still isn't, or that may never come to exist, but will still always cast a shadow on what is there.

In a way it's a religious quest, shorn of any orthodoxy. A quest of vision and sympathy, pace William Blake and Emily Dickinson, and countless other artists and poets, many mentioned above.

See also Bob Dylan. I was fourteen years old when I bought my first Dylan LP, the then-new *Another Side of Bob Dylan*. It changed everything in my life, and (I can say this with certainty now), set the course of everything that was to come. For one, I stopped being a high school math major after I started writing song lyrics in the back of geometry class. For two, I've kept at something like that ever since.

The lyric on *Another Side* that got to me most was by the then twenty-three-year-old Dylan, his head aswarm with all that the world could hold, in "Chimes of Freedom." The song is an abundance of sensory images, explosive synesthesia. Above all chimes flash like lightning bolts, but we also have echoes dissolving into light, hail hammering down, mist splattering, rain unraveling stories. Always … always that light comes at us, like arrows, like bells, like the true chimes of freedom.

As I noted above, Dylan has created innumerable brilliant photographs in his lyrics, and whole songs can be read as photobooks; but here he captures an essence of a form of my ideal photo. Indeed, from the beginning my photobook site has been called Ecstaticlightphoto, and that's because I realized early on that if I could take pictures of bells striking shadows in sounds, and all around us tolling the very chimes of freedom … wow, what a photograph! In the same museum wing as a Turner seascape, a Blake etching, a Rembrandt landscape.

"Chimes of Freedom" blew my mind; and safe to say I've been chasing those Chimes of Freedom ever since.

When I go out to take pictures, I go out with lots of ideas in my head, and as I've said, often no ideas at all … or both. But when it all comes down to it, if I can truly photograph any manifestation or even intimation of the sky cracking a poem in naked wonder, I might simply lay my camera down and walk away.

Remember Joseph Conrad, that his task is "to make you see"? As I've said, that's my task with photography, and yet there are so many levels of seeing, and if you could "see" with every sense of your body, hearing the light, speaking the sun, dancing to the beat of the shadows, tasting the clouds, smelling truth in souls walking the streets, and rhapsodizing every astonishing explosion of color in the whole wide universe … that's true seeing.

True seeing. That's what I'm always after, and when I get close, I begin to believe I just might be a photographer.

* * * * *

SO HOW DID I become a photographer? At bottom pretty simple: I found out that being a photographer was vastly more interesting than *not* being one. That walking about trying to see, and feel, as much as possible, then render all that into images was a much richer life than not doing it.

I thought being a novelist made life richer, and in many ways it did. But it kept me home, chained, as the phrase goes, to my desk. When I write, I do it every day, but I only do it till lunchtime. I learned a long time ago that anything I wrote after noon or so wouldn't hold up: not enough focus, not digging deep enough … simply, the incredible energy it takes to lift up a story and move it forward day after day dissipated after late morning. Others, of course, have different writing schedules, and I encourage any budding writer to work to discover their own. But that was mine. Only in the mornings.

Then, yes, I'd head out, usually to lunch, or at least for a long perambulation through the city. All good. Just better … so much better … with my camera, and my photographic ambitions, hanging around my neck.

So what choice did I have. Once I started taking pictures seriously, and making photobooks, I had to stick with it. It was never a hobby, never a pastime.

It was simply my life.

www.ingramcontent.com/pod-product-compliance
Lightning Source LLC
LaVergne TN
LVHW091632100826
845152LV00001B/4

* 9 7 8 1 9 3 5 5 1 2 5 7 8 *